USE WHAT YOU'VE GOT
STOP STRESSING OVER WHAT YOU DON'T HAVE

PASTOR DIANE JONES

Copyright © 2022 by Pastor Diane Jones
All rights reserved.

Published by Firebrand Publishing Atlanta, GA USA
No part of this book may be reproduced in any form or by any electronic or mechanical means, including information storage and retrieval systems, without written permission from the author, except for the use of brief quotations in a book review and certain other noncommercial uses permitted by copyright law.

For permission requests, write to the publisher, addressed "Attention: Permissions coordinator," at the email address: support@firebrandpublishing.com
Scripture quotations taken from the KING JAMES VERSION (KJV): KING JAMES VERSION, public domain.

Firebrand Publishing publishes in a variety of print and electronic formats and by print-on-demand. For more information about Firebrand Publishing products, visit https://firebrandpublishing.com

ISBN: 978-1-941907-54-2 (paperback)
ISBN: 978-1-941907-53-5 (ebook)

Printed in the United States of America

CONTENTS

Acknowledgment   v
Preface   vii

1. How My Book Was Birthed   1
2. My Testimony   4
3. Things That Keep Us On Track   8
4. When I Was Younger   13
5. Use What You Got   18
6. Sometimes All We Need   21
7. Forget Not All His Benefits   27
8. If You Don't USE What You Got   32

About the Author   35

ACKNOWLEDGMENT

I thank God my Father and his Son, Jesus Christ, my savior and my comforter, which is The Holy Ghost, for allowing me to write this book. It's been on the back burner long enough, as they say, but I realized that now is the time to go forth.

I thank my husband for understanding that I had this goal pressing on my heart to write and have this book published. It was lot of time spent alone, but it was worth it.

I thank my church family for having confidence in me as their Pastor, giving me strength in knowing that I could do this and encouraging me to go forth with it.

I'm grateful for all the people that God has put into my life to help make this all possible.

I'm really and truly grateful for my family that sticks right by my side in every way.

PREFACE

God had impressed on my heart for a while to write this book, and I believe that it will be a blessing to everyone who reads it. I have preached this topic many times at different churches and 'till this day, people are still talking about how much of a blessing it was to hear... I hope the same for you. "Use What You Got."

HOW MY BOOK WAS BIRTHED

$\mathcal{I}$ have always liked making ladies' Prayer lap scarfs/handkerchiefs with lace. One day, I wanted to make more, only to find that I didn't have the specific colors of lace that I wanted to use.

Then I heard, *In every area of my life, I have learned to use what I have and to be content.*

Paul says it this way in Philippians 4:11, "Not that I speak in respect of want: for I have learned, in whatsoever state I am, therewith to be content.

"12: I know both how to be abased, and I know how to abound: every where and in all things I am instructed both to be full and to be hungry, both to abound and to suffer need."

But, I have personally learned myself in Philippians 4:13, "I can do all things through Christ which strengtheneth me."

As I began to write this book, I made up my mind to stay focused and get my book written, so that it can be published this year. I believe that God wants me to stay focused as He has allowed me to not only purchase a Ford Focus in 2005 and kept it for 6 years, but also be able to trade it in 2011 for another.

That is a blessing within itself. Through the purchasing of both vehicles, I could see that God has continuously reminded me to keep focused, leaving me determined in doing so.

As I was watching a Pastor on 'Word Network', I discovered that she had just published her book. Like me, she had procrastinated for some years, until the moment that she made up her mind to do it. She started in January 2018 and was ready to publish by the end of February 2018.

Her story really inspired me to know that I can do it also. I'm trying with all of my heart to keep the word procrastination out of my vocabulary. I find myself truly understanding what the mother of Jesus said when they ran out of wine for the marriage in Cana of Galilee.

John 2:3, "And when they wanted wine, the mother of Jesus saith unto him, They have no wine.

"4: Jesus saith her, Woman, what have I to do with

thee? mine hour is not yet come. His mother saith unto the servants, Whatsoever he saith unto you, do it."

I'm trying to do the things that I have planned. If I plan it, I, with the help of the Lord, tries to make it happen. I remind myself to stop planning if I'm not going to put it into action. God lets me know through his word in: Isaiah 54:17, "No weapon that is formed against thee shall prosper; and every tongue that shall rise against thee in judgment thou shalt condemn. This is the heritage of the servants of the Lord, and their righteousness is of me, saith the Lord."

MY TESTIMONY

I love the Lord with all of my heart, mind, body, spirit and soul. In other words, ALL of me loves the Lord. God saved me years ago and I'm still running for my life.

If anybody asked, 'What's the matter with you?'

I tell them, I am Saved, Sanctified, Holy Ghost filled, and running for my life. I have a crown waiting for me, and if I give up now, I won't get it. But, I served a notice to the Devil, Satan, the deceiver that I am not about to give up. God has been good to me and has brought me from a mighty long way. As a matter of fact, He's blessing me right now and I have come too far for my journey to end.

I would like to tell you my testimony about my life before the Lord saved me. I was doing some of everything that I felt that I was grown enough to do. I was drinking, smoking and partying so much that I thought I was having a good time.

But, the honest truth was that I was tired of what I was doing. I prayed unto the Lord and said, "Lord, I'm tired of the kind of life that I am living."

Getting high every day and partying was just too much and I needed a change. There was nothing about what I was doing that was positive. I knew that life was supposed to be better than the life that I was living.

God heard my prayer.

One day my ex-sister-in-law, along with her Pastor knocked on my door. I answered it, asked them in, and I showed them great hospitality. Then they began to tell me that Jesus loved me, but He didn't love what I was doing. That He was able to deliver me from the things that I was doing and to save me.

Just knowing that Jesus loved me, was the best news that I had ever heard. I didn't get saved then, but what they said to me stayed with me. When they came back to visit me, I told them that I was in the same boat that I was in the last time that they came. I was still drinking and smoking, but they insisted to tell me more about Jesus. It's safe to say that they were real women of God.

New Year's Resolutions. We mean well when we make them. Jesus puts it like this in Matthew 26:41, "Watch and Pray, that ye enter not into temptation: the spirit indeed is willing, but the flesh is weak."

So, that is why it is hard for us to keep our new year

resolutions. But, on January 1, 1980 I kept my 'New Year Resolution.' It doesn't matter where you are, it just takes a made-up mind.

I was at work in the break room at Piccadilly Cafeteria, when it was in Military Circle Mall, where I was employed at that time. It was a New Year's Day. I said "Lord, I know that you sent for me two times by those young ladies, but you don't have to send for me a third time because on this day, I'm giving my life to you. Those habits that I had, take it away from me."

God removed the habit, the taste of smoking and drinking from me.

According to the word in Romans 10:8-11, "But what saith it? The word is nigh thee, even in thy mouth, and in thy heart: that is, the word of faith, which we preach;

"9: That if thou confess with thy mouth the Lord Jesus, and shalt believe in thine heart that God hath raised him from the dead, thou shalt be saved.

"10: For with the heart man believeth unto righteousness; and with the mouth confession is made unto salvation. So, that day I also believeth in my heart, and confessed with my mouth that I was saved and had given my life to the Lord."

When one of my co-workers invited me to Church, I decided to start working on my soul salvation in the Lord.

Since then, have I crossed every T and dotted every I? The answer is, no. Sometimes in my writing I forget to cross my T's and dot my I's. But, thanks be to God who gives me the victory through Jesus Christ our Lord. He is still moulding me and shaping me into what he wants me to be.

1 John 3:1 says, "Behold, what manner of love the Father hath bestowed upon us, that we should be called the sons of God: therefore the world knoweth us not, because it knew him not.

"2: Beloved, now we are the sons of God, and it doth not yet appear what we shall be: but we know that, when he shall appear, we shall be like him; for we shall see him as he is.

"3: And every man that hath this hope in him purifieth himself, even as he is pure."

I love living this kind of life. It's a blessed life, a good life and a holy life. I'm living to live again with God in Heaven where the streets are paved with pure gold.

THINGS THAT KEEP US ON TRACK

STUDYING THE WORD OF GOD

> "Study to shew thyself approved unto God a workman that needeth not to be ashamed, rightly dividing the word of truth. Praying without Ceasing."
>
> — 2 TIMOTHY 2:15

> "Pray Without Ceasing."
>
> — 1 THESSALONIANS 5:17

*A*ll through the word of God, we are encouraged to always pray and not to faint. Someone even wrote it in a song. *'Don't stop Praying,* *because the Lord is near, Don't stop Praying, because he will hear your cry, the Lord has promised and his word is true. Don't stop Praying because he will answer you.'*

Jesus took the time to teach the disciples to Pray.

"After this manner therefore Pray ye:
Our Father which art in heaven, Hallowed be thy name.

Thy kingdom come, Thy will be done in earth, as it is in heaven.

Give us this day our daily bread.

And forgive us our debts, as we forgive our debtors.

And lead us not into temptation, but deliver us from evil:

For thine is Kingdom, and the power, and the glory, for ever.

Amen.

— MATTHEW 6:9-13

I know that we usually stop here, but check out verses 14 & 15.

"For if ye forgive men their trespasses, your heavenly Father will also forgive you."

— MATTHEW 6:14

But, this is what a lot of people miss in the next verse.

"But, if ye forgive not men their trespasses, neither will your Father forgive your trespasses."

— MATTHEW 6:15

FASTING

17: "But thou, when thou fastest, anoint thine head, and wash thy face;

18: "That thou appear not unto men to fast, but unto thy Father which is in secret: and thy Father, which seeth in secret, shall reward thee openly."

— MATTHEW 6:17-18

6: "Is not this the fast that I have chosen? to loose the bands of wickedness, to undo the heavy burdens, and to let the oppressed go free, and that ye break every yoke?

7: " Is it not to deal thy bread to the hungry, and

that thou bring the poor that are cast out to thy house? when thou seest the naked, that thou cover him; and that thou hide not thyself from thine own flesh?

8: "Then shall thy light break forth as the morning, and thine health shall spring forth speedily: and thy righteousness shall go before thee; the glory of the Lord shall be thy reward.

9: "Then shall thou call, and the Lord shall answer; thou shalt cry, and he shall say, Here I am. If thou take away from the midst of thee the yoke, the putting forth of the finger, and speaking vanity;"

— ISAIAH 58:6-9

Then you can hear what the spirit is saying unto the church.

PRAISING HIM

"Praise ye the Lord, Praise the Lord, O my Soul.

"While I live will I Praise the Lord: I will sing Praises unto my God while I have any being."

— PSALM 146:1-2

I have also learned to do what the word says in Proverbs 3:5-6.

> 5: "Trust in the Lord with all thine heart; and lean not to thine own understanding.
>
> 6: "In all thy ways acknowledge him, and he shall direct thy paths."

— PROVERBS 3:5-6

When you give your whole life to the Lord, there's no problem doing what he says, even if you don't always understand it.

Sometimes when we ask God for things, we try to figure out how He's going to do it. But, that's not our responsibility to try and discover how He's going to work it out. It is our responsibility to believe.

> "For with God nothing shall be impossible."

— LUKE 1:37

WHEN I WAS YOUNGER

When I was younger, I attended the New Willow Grove Baptist Church, where Rev. Terry Wingate was the Pastor at that time. He would sing a song almost every Sunday.

'Everlasting life is Free
I'm so glad,
Jesus gave to me everlasting life.'

I didn't know what everlasting life was, but the way he sang that song, I really wanted to know what everlasting life was. He sang it with the power of the holy ghost, and if you didn't have it, you wanted it.

Now, I can say that I have gained everlasting life. What a wonderful change Jesus has made in my life.

We did not have all the luxuries of life, so my mother and father learned to use what they had and made the best of it. We had a large family of 10 and by the grace of God we made it and are still making it.

Our bath tubs during these early years was the #2 tubs. The #2 tubs along with the wash board was used for washing our clothes in one and rinse in another. Then, hanging them on the clothes line outside and sometimes inside. We didn't have a washing machine.

We also had a pump where we got our water out of. We had to save water to pour into it so that we could prime it.

We had the black telephone with a ring dial and it was a party line, which meant that we had 2 to 3 people on one line.

We had a black and white television, and a record player that my aunt saved up green stamps to get one Christmas. It played 45 rpm and 33 rpm records. Don't forget the 8 track tape player and 8 track tapes, the cassette tape player and cassettes.

Wait, I know that I may have lost a lot of my readers, because I know you may not have heard of all of this, but a lot of us have lived with the same things that I did. We had school clothes, church clothes, and black & white shoes that lasted a long time. Our mother would stay up late nights sewing clothes so that my sisters and I would have something to wear to school the next day.

We would have hand me down clothes and my mother would go to the goodwill store and buy clothes for our brothers also. We also had school shoes and church shoes.

My mother would wash, and plait our hair when we were younger. But as we got older, she decided to wash, straighten and curl our hair.

She would cook soups, stews, beans & biscuits, which was one of my favorite foods and still is. Fried chicken with gravy and mac & cheese was our Sunday treat. So, all I'm saying is that they used what they had.

Exodus 4:2 says, "And the Lord said unto him, (Moses) What is that in thine hand? And he said, A rod.

"3: And he said, Cast it on the ground. And he cast it on the ground, and it became a serpent; and Moses fled from before it.

"4: And the Lord said unto Moses, put forth thine hand, and take it by the tail. And he put forth his hand, and caught it, and it became a rod in his hand."

God allowed Moses to use that same rod that was in his hand to part the red sea.

Exodus 14:27-30

"27: And Moses stretched forth his hand over the sea, and the sea returned to his strength when the morning appeared; and the Egyptians fled against it; and the Lord overthrew the Egyptians in the midst of the sea.

"28: And the waters returned, and covered the chariots, and the horsemen, and all the host of Pharaoh that came into the sea after them; there remained not so much as one of them.

"29: But the children of Israel walked upon dry land in the midst of the sea; and the waters were a wall unto them on their right hand, and on their left.

"30: Thus the Lord saved Israel that day out of the hand of Egyptians; and Israel saw the Egyptians dead upon the sea shore."

That rod in Moses' hand was just what God allowed him to use to defeat the enemy.

The point that I want to make is to say that we can't give into the devil every time you feel that you don't have what you think that you need to get the job done. God allowed Moses to use what he had in his hand which was a rod. I know little becomes much when you put it in the master's hand.

Sometimes, we have pain and we want to stay home from church, but that's the place that we need to go, so that we can get healed. This may sound simple, but it is true. Sometimes we stay home from church because we don't have what we think we need to wear.

Sometimes, different events or programs have been planned at our churches and you are asked to wear a certain color of which some of us don't have and we stay home. The head of the event or programs should let you know that this is the colors that we are asked to

USE WHAT YOU'VE GOT

wear, but if you don't have these colors, please don't stay home, wear what you got.

But, if the truth be told some of us have enough clothes and shoes to start a small thrift store. In other words, we need to keep it moving.

USE WHAT YOU GOT

I'm reminded of how Elisha showed the woman how to pay her debt in 2 Kings 4:1-7,

"1: Now there cried a certain woman of the wives of the sons of the prophets unto Elisha, saying, thy servant my husband is dead; and thou knowest that thy servant did fear the lord: and the creditor is come to take unto him my two sons to be bondmen.

"2: And Elisha said unto her, What shall I do for thee? tell me, what hast thou in the house? And she said, Thine handmaid hath not any thing in the house, save a pot of oil.

"3: Then he said, Go, borrow thee vessels abroad of all thy neighbours, even empty vessels; borrow not a few."

. . .

USE WHAT YOU'VE GOT

In other words, he was saying unto her to borrow as many as you can because the more you get the more money you will make.

"4: And when thou art come in, thou shalt shut the door upon thee and upon thy sons, and shalt pour out into all those vessels, and thou shalt set aside that which is full." (2 Kings 4:4)

I was wondering why he told her to shut the door. I think it was to keep all the nosey neigbours out, because no doubt, the talk was already starting when she borrowed vessels from neighbor number one, two, three, four, and so on. It's back to neighbor number one and she wants to know what she wants with so many vessels that she has to borrow from the whole neighborhood.

That's why 1 Thessalonians 4:11 says, "And that ye study to be quiet, and to do your own business, and to work with your own hands, as we commanded you;
"12: That ye may walk honestly toward them that are without, and that ye may have lack of nothing."

Now back to the widow woman,

"6: And it came to pass, when the vessels were full, that she said unto her son, Bring me yet a vessel. And he said unto her, there is not a vessel more. And the oil stayed.

"7: Then she came and told the man of God. And he said, 'go, sell the oil, and pay thy debt, and live thou and thy children of the rest.'" (2 Kings 4:6-7)

What you have to understand here is that you can get what you need. When you begin to 'use what you got', like Elisha, you can have enough to live off and to pay your bills. So, you don't have to keep stressing on what you don't have.

Use what you got.

SOMETIMES ALL WE NEED

PRAYER

Samson had one more prayer left and that was in Judges 16:28, "And Samson called unto the Lord, and said O Lord God, remember me, I pray thee, and strengthen me, I pray thee, only this once, O God, that I may be at once avenged of the Philistines for my two eyes.

"29: And Samson took hold of the two middle pillars upon which the house stood, and on which it was borne up, of the one with his right hand, and of the other with his left.

"30: And Samson said, Let me die with the Philistines. And he bowed himself with all his might; and the house fell upon all the lords, and upon all the people that were therein. So the dead which he slew at his death were more than they which he slew in his life."

PRAISE

Believe me, praise will be the breakthrough that you need. When the armies had come up against Jehoshaphat, all they had was another Praise. In 2 Chronicles 20:21- 22,

"21: And when he had consulted with the people, he appointed singers unto the Lord, and that should praise the beauty of holiness, as they went out before the army, and to say, Praise the Lord; for his mercy endureth for ever.

"22: And when they began to sing and to praise, the Lord set ambushments against the children of Ammon, Moab, and mount Seir, which were come against Judah; and they were smitten.

"23: For the children of Ammon and Moab stood up against the inhabitants of mount Seir, utterly to slay and destroy them: and when they had made an end of the inhabitants of Seir, every one helped to destroy another."

SONG

Psalm 32:7 says, "Thou art my hiding place; thou shalt preserve me from trouble; thou shalt compass me about with songs of deliverance. Selah."

The song may be Al-le-lu-ia anyhow, don't let problems get you down. If troubles come your way, lift your head and say Al-le-lu-ia anyhow.

When we look back over our life, we find ourselves singing another song. If it had not been for the Lord who was on our side, where would I be, or maybe, Jesus.

I'll never forget what you've done for me. How can I forget how you set me free, or maybe, The blood that Jesus shed for me on Calvary, that gives me strength from day to day will never lose it's Power, or maybe it's I'm free, no longer bound, no more chain holding me, my soul is resting, it's just another blessing. Praise the Lord, Al-lu-le-ia, I'm free.

WORD

PSALM 46:10 says, "Be still, and know that I am God: I will be exalted among the heathen, I will be exalted in the earth."

Or, Isaiah 41:10, "Fear thou not; for I am with thee: be not dismayed; for I am thy God: I will strengthen thee; yea, I will help thee; yea, I will uphold thee with the right hand of my righteousness."

Maybe, John 14 :27, "Peace I leave with you, my peace I give unto you: not as the world giveth, give I unto you. Let not your heart be troubled, neither let it be afraid."

. . .

That's why when life seems to deal you a lemon, learn to make lemonade. Don't let the devil steal your joy. For the joy of the Lord is your strength.

John 10:10 says, "The thief cometh not, but for to steal, and to kill, and to destroy: I am come that they might have life, and that they might have it more abundantly."

The devil wants to steal your joy, he wants to kill your character and to destroy your life.

Galatians 3:1 says, "O foolish Galatians, who hath bewitched you, that ye should not obey the truth, before whose eyes Jesus Christ hath been evidently set forth, crucified among you?"
Galatians 3:3 says, "Are you so foolish? having begun in the Spirit, are ye now made perfect by the flesh?"
Galatians 5:7 says, "Ye did run well; who did hinder you that ye should not obey the truth?"

That's why it is good to know and receive God for yourself because no one can hinder you, but you. It's nice to know that psalm 27:1 says, "The Lord is my

USE WHAT YOU'VE GOT

light and my salvation; whom shall I fear? The Lord is the strength of my life; of whom shall I be afraid?"

Psalm 24:7-10 says, "Lift up your heads, O ye gates; and be ye lift up, ye everlasting doors; and the King of glory shall come in.

"8: Who is this King of glory? The Lord strong and mighty, the Lord mighty in battle.

"9: Lift up your heads, O ye gates; even lift them up, ye everlasting doors; and the King of glory shall come in.

"10: Who is this King of glory? The Lord of hosts, he is the King of glory. Selah."

Sometimes we have to be still and let the Lord fight our battles.

2 Chronicles 20:17 says, "Ye shall not need to fight in this battle: set yourselves, stand ye still, and see the salvation of the Lord with you, O Judah and Jerusalem: fear not, nor be dismayed; to morrow go out against them: for the Lord will be with you."

As long as you have the Lord with you, what do you have to worry about? That's why David says, Psalm 27:13, "I had fainted, unless I had believed to see the goodness of the Lord in the land of the living."

. . .

For this reason, I always ask the Lord to lead me and guide me along the way, because if he leads and guides me, I shall not stray. Let me walk with thee each day and draw me closer to thee.

James 4:7 says, "Submit yourselves therefore to God. Resist the devil, and he will flee from you."

James 7:10 says, "Humble yourselves in the sight of the Lord, and he shall lift you up."

It is important for us all to continue to live right and walk right and to speak the truth in our heart. God will take care of you and he will see you through any situation.

FORGET NOT ALL HIS BENEFITS

David says in: Pslam 103:1-5

"1: Bless the Lord, O my soul: and all that is within me, bless his holy name.
"2: Bless the Lord, O my soul, and forget not all his benefits:
"3: Who forgiveth all thine inquities; who healeth thy diseases;
"4: Who redeemeth thy life from destruction; who crowneth thee with lovingkindness and tender mercies;
"5: Who satisfieth thy mouth with good things; so that thy youth is renewed like the eagle's.

Psalm 68:19 says, Blessed be the Lord, who daily loadeth us with benefits even the God of our salvation."

Then David says in Psalm 116:12, "What shall I render unto the Lord for all his benefits toward me?"

I made up in my mind that I will praise him for all the great things that he has done for me. God is awesome in all his ways, can't nobody do you like the Lord.

I have been working on this book as the Lord gives it to me. Chapter by chapter. As I write this, we are in the middle part of September 2018, where we have been under a hurricane warning by the name of Florence. It was a category 4, with up to 140 mph winds that was headed to the east coast where we live. But, with much prayer, the Lord caused it to turn, downgrading the hurricane to a category 3, then to a category 2 and eventually to a 1 by the time it actually hit landfall in Wilmington, North Carolina. The Lord caused the hurricane to go down to a tropical storm strength. God worked a Miracle.

If it had stayed like it was, there would have been a lot more destruction than what it was. But, it was sad to know that some did lose their life because of the storm. So, we continue to pray for the families who did lose loved ones and that were flooded out.

I had to add this to my book because we have to remember what the Lord has done for us.

· · ·

Lamentations 3:22 says, "It is of the Lord's mercies that we are not consumed, because his compassions fail not.

"23: They are new every morning: great is thy faithfulness."

Jesus loves me this I know because the Bible tells me so.

John 3:16 says, "For God so loved the world, that he gave his only begotton son, that whosoever believeth in him should not perish, but have eternal life."

For many of us, this was something that we all learned in Sunday school. Well, all the ones that went to Sunday school. We had to go, or else we couldn't go anywhere else. So, I went and after going I actually fell in love with it and still am. Sunday school is something that I don't miss. Someone put it like this, "If you know everything, Sunday school needs you, but if you don't know everything, you need Sunday school."

Well, I have come to the end of my book and I pray that it has been a blessing to you as it has been to me in writing it. I want to encourage everyone that read this book, according to 1 Corinthians 2:9, "But as it is written, Eye hath not seen, nor ear heard, neither have entered into the heart of man, the things which God hath prepared for them that love him."

And I know that you love the Lord and his people, so, just hold on, wait and see how God does just what he says. It is important to write down the things that you desire from the Lord.

Habakkuk 2:2-3 says it like this,
"2: And the Lord answered me, and said, Write the vision, and make it plain upon tables, that he may run that readeth it.
"3: For the vision is yet for an appointed time, but at the end it shall speak, and not lie: though it tarry, wait for it; because it will surely come, it will not tarry."

I was looking at a clip from Steve Harvey. His teacher asked him what he wanted to do when they got older. Steve Harvey wrote that he wanted to be on television and the teacher thought that he was being smart, and she let his parents know that he was being difficult. But, that was what he wanted to do. His parents asked him to go to his room.

His father came in and asked Steve what the teacher wanted to see. Steve said that she wanted to see him write, play basketball or football. So, his father told him to write it down what the teacher suggested and give it to his teacher.

But, the paper that he wanted to be on television, keep it in your drawer and every morning before you go to school read it and every day that you come from school, read it.

Steve Harvey is on television every day of the week. He held onto what he wanted to do and it happened. That inspired me because Steve didn't give up on his dreams no matter what anyone said or did to stray him away from his goals.

You can be whatever you want to be with the help of others and of course the Lord. You be blessed and watch out for my next book, because it's on the way.

"To God Be The Glory."

IF YOU DON'T USE WHAT YOU GOT

- If Moses had not been obedient to God and use what he had, which was the rod that was in his hand, the children of Israel would not have been able to cross the Red Sea on dry land.
- If I had not used the material and lace that I already had on hand, I would not have been able to make about one dozen of lap scarfs and handkerchiefs.
- If the widow woman had not been obedient to the man of God, in borrowing vessels, filling them up with oil and selling them, she would not have had the money to pay her bills and to live off the rest.
- If we wear the clothes that we have, that will open the door up for more.

- Psalm 27:14 says, "Wait on the lord: be of good courage, and he shall strengthen thine heart: wait, I say on the lord."
- When there is a purchase that you are about to make, and the lord says wait, not now, if you are obedient and wait on the thing that you were about to purchase, whether it be a house, car, or large appliances, the lord will allow it to go on sale.
- If God leads you in a different way than you usually go to work and you follow his leading and find out when you get to work that it was a bad accident the way that you usually go to work and you say to the lord, 'now I see why you lead me in another direction today.'
- So, if we don't learn, sometimes to use what we got, we can miss seeing the blessing of God in our life and on our life. Because God can bless the little that you have, and it becomes more.
- A good example is St. Luke 9:13, "But he said unto them, Give ye them to eat. And they said, 'We have no more but five loaves and two fishes; except we should go and buy meat for all this people.'
- "14: For they were about five thousand men. And he said to his disciples, 'make them all sit down by fifties in a company.'

- "15: And they did so, and made them all sit down,
- "16: Then he took the five loaves and the two fishes, and looking up to heaven, he blessed them, and brake, and gave to the disciples to set before the multitude.
- "17: And they did all eat, and were all filled: and there was taken up of fragments that remained to them twelve baskets."

ABOUT THE AUTHOR

Pastor Diane Jones received Jesus Christ as her personal saviour in 1980. Pastor Jones has ministered to spiritual needs of assisted living seniors, and served the incarcerated in spiritual ministry, in the City of Chesapeake, Virginia.

Her many capacities of service to the church include Usher, Missionary, Sunday School Teacher, and for 10 years, as a licensed Minister at Peace Temple Church of Deliverance. For the last 2 years along with her husband Delano Jones, she's served Philippians Church of Christ Holy Disciples.

Diane and Delano live in the beautiful city of Chesapeake, Virginia. Her love for people, and the lord confirms that whosoever believes in Jesus, should not perish, and have everlasting life.

www.ingramcontent.com/pod-product-compliance
Lightning Source LLC
Chambersburg PA
CBHW012007120526
44592CB00040B/2658